STEVE
YOUNG

(Photo on front cover.)

Steve Young prepares to pass.

(Photo on previous pages.)

Young looks for an open receiver.

Text copyright © 1997 by The Child's World, Inc.
All rights reserved. No part of this book may be reproduced
or utilized in any form or by any means without written
permission from the Publisher.
Printed in the United States of America.

Photography supplied by Wide World Photos Inc.

Library of Congress Catalog-in-Publication Data
Rambeck, Richard.
Steve Young / Richard Rambeck
p. cm.
Summary: Relates this San Francisco quarterback's march to the
1994 Super Bowl, where he threw a record six touchdown passes
and made the fastest opening score in Super Bowl history.
ISBN 1-56766-264-1 (Lib.Bdg.)

1. Young, Steve, 1961 — Juvenile literature. 2. Football players —
United States — Biography — Juvenile lliterature.
3. San Francisco 49ers (Football team. [1. Young,Steve, 1961.
2. Football players. 3. San Francisco 49ers (Football team).]
I. Title
GV939.Y69R68   1997   95-44600
796.332'092 — dc20   CIP
[B]   AC

STEVE
YOUNG

BY RICHARD RAMBECK

Steve Young was mad. No, he was furious! And Steve Young doesn't get angry very often. It was 1994, and Young had been taken out of an early season game between his team, the San Francisco 49ers, and the Philadelphia Eagles. The 49ers were losing 33–8, which was bad enough. But what made it worse was that San Francisco coach George Seifert substituted for Young while the 49ers had the ball. That meant that Young had to leave the huddle when another quarterback came in to replace him.

No professional athlete wants to leave a game that way. After the 40–8 San Francisco loss, Seifert admitted he had made a mistake in pulling Young out like that. Seifert wasn't benching Young. Actually, the 49er coach just wanted to make sure that his star quarterback didn't get hurt in a game that was already lost. But Young was still mad, and he told Seifert so. He told a lot of people, in fact. But Young's teammates and the San Francisco coaches were glad to see him get angry!

Young can even complete a pass from his knees.

Steve Young might be too nice a guy, some people thought. After all, a quarterback is a team leader, and leaders need to take charge. In football, sometimes that can mean getting mad, yelling at teammates, urging them to do better. Young was the leader of one of the best

teams in the National Football League. Still, the 49ers hadn't won a Super Bowl with Young as their starting quarterback. Joe Montana had led the team to four Super Bowl victories, the last in 1990.

Steve Young had done pretty much everything he could in pro football—except win a Super Bowl. According to NFL statistics, he was the best quarterback in the history of pro football. In the 1993 season, he threw for more than 4,000 yards, something Montana never did in his career. He also threw 183 passes in a row without an interception. Even so, San Francisco wasn't the National Football Conference team that played in the Super Bowl that season. Dallas was.

11

When the 1994 season began, San Francisco fans wondered whether Steve Young could finally pass his team into the Super Bowl. Early in the year, it didn't look good. The 49ers went to Kansas City and lost 24–17 to the Chiefs, whose quarterback was a guy named Joe Montana. With two key offensive linemen hurt and unable to play, Young spent most of the game running for his life. The Chiefs punished Young, who even got sick on the sideline.

After the loss to Philadelphia, the 49ers were 3–2, hardly the record of a Super Bowl contender. But now Steve Young was mad. For the rest of the season, he played as well as any quarterback

Young goes for a 12-yard gain against the Los Angeles Raiders.

12

has ever played. The 49er offense, which was good to begin with, became almost unstoppable. "We have always had an offense that could put points on the board," said 49er receiver Jerry Rice. "But with this offense, it's something different. I think it has to do with Steve Young."

Late in the season, Dallas came to San Francisco to play the 49ers. It was a very important game because the winner would probably wind up playing the NFC championship game at home. In 1993, San Francisco had to go to Dallas for the NFC title game. Dallas won 30–21. The 49ers believed they could beat Dallas in 1994, but they wanted to play the NFC title game at home. Young had an outstanding game against the Cowboys, leading San Francisco to a 21–14 victory.

The tough Dallas defense couldn't stop Young. He rushed for 60 yards on eight carries and threw a 57-yard touchdown pass to Rice, putting San Francisco ahead 14–7. Helped by their victory over Dallas, the 49ers posted the best record in the NFC. That meant that San Francisco would play all its NFC play-off games at home. Young finished the 1994 season with 35 touchdown passes and only 10 interceptions. He threw for 3,969 yards and completed more than 70 percent of his passes.

Young decides to run on this play against Dallas.

"I feel like I'm in total control," Young said. "This offense has the answers to anything anybody does defensively." After an easy win over Chicago in their first playoff game, the 49ers faced Dallas in the NFC title game. San Francisco's defense forced Dallas to make mistakes that helped give the 49ers a 21–0 first-quarter lead. Young threw two touchdown passes and ran for another score. San Francisco won 38–28. Steve Young was going to the Super Bowl.

The experts gave the AFC champion San Diego Chargers almost no chance of beating Young and the 49ers in the Super Bowl. San Francisco was favored to win by $19\frac{1}{2}$ points, the largest point spread in Super Bowl history. It didn't take the 49ers long to prove the experts right. On the third play after receiving the opening kickoff, Young hit Rice with a 44-yard TD pass. The game was only 1 minute, 24 seconds old. It was the fastest opening score in Super Bowl history.

A fter San Diego punted, Young led the 49ers on a quick 79-yard march down the field. The key plays were a 21-yard run by Young and a 51-yard TD pass to running back Ricky Watters. After five minutes of Super Bowl XXIX, San Francisco was ahead 14–0. But Young and the 49ers were just getting started. Young threw a Super Bowl record six touch-

Young plows up the middle against San Diego.

down passes as San Francisco rolled to a 49–26 victory. Young was also the game's leading rusher, with 49 yards on five carries.

"That is probably the best offense that people will see in their lifetime," said 49er center Jesse Sapolu. Steve Young was a major reason for that. "Is this great or what?" Young said. "I mean, I haven't thrown six touchdown passes in a game in my life. Then I throw six in the Super Bowl. Unbelievable." After years of trying and coming close, Young finally had won a Super Bowl. "This,"he said in the happy 49er locker room,"is the greatest feeling in the world."